IMAGES
of Sport

HUNSLET
RUGBY LEAGUE CLUB
1883-1973

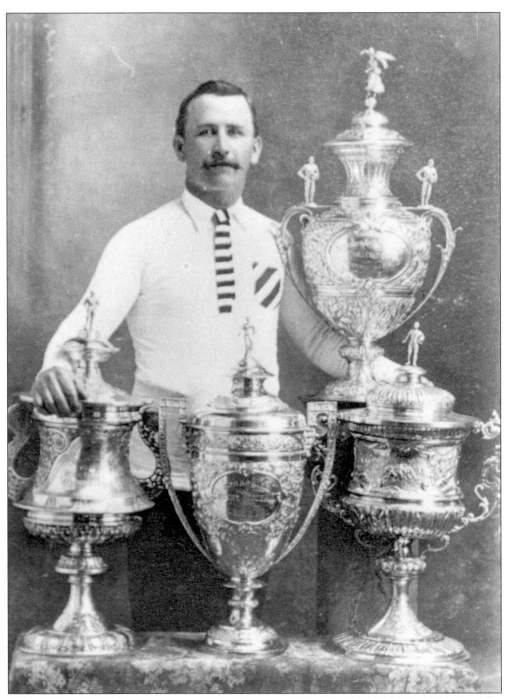

Albert Edward Goldthorpe was one of the first stars of the Hunslet club. 'Ahr Albert', as the crowds at Parkside called him, made his debut in October 1888 and was soon renowned for his goal-kicking abilities, kicking 14 goals from 15 attempts in a game against Dudley Hill in 1890. He was thirty-six when his beloved Hunslet won 'all four cups' in 1908 and during the season became the first player to kick over 100 goals in a season. Often described as the 'Prince of Goalkickers', Albert kicked well over 800 in his career with Hunslet, his first and only club.

IMAGES
of Sport

HUNSLET
RUGBY LEAGUE CLUB
1883-1973

Compiled by
Les Hoole

TEMPUS

Tempus Publishing Limited
The Mill, Brimscombe Port,
Stroud, Gloucestershire, GL5 2QG

ISBN 0 7524 1641 3

Typesetting and origination by
Tempus Publishing Limited
Printed in Great Britain by
Midway Clark Printing, Wiltshire

The Hunslet badge which was based on the coat of arms of the Hunslet Board of Guardians, the body responsible for welfare and education in Hunslet. The motto *Nihil sine deo* translates to 'Nothing without God'.

Contents

Introduction   7

Acknowledgements   8

1.   Formation and the Northern Union   9

2.   All Four Cups   29

3.   Between the Wars   45

4.   Wembley '34   61

5.   The All Leeds Final   69

6.   Derby Days   77

7.   The Forties and Fifties   89

8.   The Sixties and Closure   113

Jack Walkington, the Hunslet captain and full-back, who played a huge part in the Parksiders' successful campaigns of the thirties.

Introduction

'It has been a working man's club since its formation and is today. The club was founded by working men, and has been the working men's pride to develop and manage it throughout'.

These few words, spoken by one of the founder members of the Hunslet club twenty years after it had been formed, hold the key to the club's character and traditions. The club continued the democratic views and deeds of those visionary men of the 1880s for many years and it was only in the latter part of the club's history that those virtues were forgotten – with disastrous consequences. The Hunslet club always prided itself on its sense of community and the great links it had with the local schools and workshops. These bonds and the depth of feeling they created saw many fine players plucked from within a small radius of the Parkside ground, strengthening the ties with the local area.

Success came to Hunslet several times during the days at Parkside and the Parksiders were, on several occasions, one of the finest clubs in the game, winning each of the major trophies available. Several of the 'home grown' players gained county and international honours and many left Hunslet for highly successful careers with leading clubs.

During the late 1960s and early '70s, a rapid decline in the game as whole was heightened considerably at Hunslet with the closure of many of the local factories and wholesale clearance of the old housing around the ground. The very area from which Hunslet drew their support was being torn down and huge numbers of people were moving away from the South Leeds area. The changes had a disastrous effect on the club: attendance's dwindled and a series of player strikes and off the field disputes began to tear the heart out of the club. Amidst this internal turmoil secret plans were being made to sell the Parkside grounds and either relocate or close the club. In 1972 the unthinkable finally happened and Parkside was sold to a development company. The following year Hunslet played their last game at Parkside and within months were officially closed down.

A 'new' Hunslet Rugby League Football Club was formed from the ashes and betrayals of the old club and thanks to a new generation of players and passionate officials the great name lives on. The club is now based in a new purpose-built stadium a stone's throw from the original Parkside ground. The story of Hunslet from 1973 to the present day is also a fascinating one. Both on and off the field of play it is a tale of deep determination, hope, expectation and eventual success. This book does not represent a definitive history nor a complete photographic record of the Hunslet Cricket, Football and Athletic Club, but these images are a celebration of the club, its deeds, successes, failures, players and followers for the ninety-five years that they played at Woodhouse Hill and Parkside. Research into all aspects of the history of Hunslet, and indeed any other club, is an ongoing project and I would be very interested to hear of any photographs, cuttings and general memorabilia, especially that connected with the 1973-1999 period.

Les Hoole
(14 Penfield Road, Drighlington, Bradford. BD11 1ES)

Acknowledgements

The majority of the images in this book have been collected over a long period of time and during those years I have had the help and support (and made good friends) of several dedicated ex-players, collectors, writers and historians. I must thank, in no particular order: Tim Auty, Mike Green, Robert Gate, Andy Hudson, Dave Makin, Ben, Dianne and Verity Hoole, Phillip Harrison, Barry Pepper, Cliff Pearson and Rene Hoole, Geoff Gunney, Billy Baldwinson, Harry Jepson, Sam Newbound, the late Jack Walkington, Steve Calline, Trevor Delaney, Steve Brady (editor of *The Rugby Leaguer*), Norma Harding, Hunslet RLFC, Alf Barron, Charlie Baxter and the staff at Bradford Central Reference Library.

One

Formation and the Northern Union

Billy Gilston was one of the driving forces behind the formation of Hunslet RLFC. He had played for two of the leading Hunslet-based football clubs, Albion and Excelsior, and saw the opportunity for the clubs to merge when an Association Football club that played at Woodhouse Hill folded. A grant of £30 was obtained from the Hunslet Cricket Club, who rented the ground from the landlord of the nearby Cemetery Tavern (now called the Parnaby), and the Hunslet Rugby Club was formed on 21 May 1883.

Hunslet initially played in blue-and-white-quartered shirts but soon changed to their famous white shirts with a chocolate coloured badge. Rent increases on the Woodhouse Hill ground forced the fledgling club to move to Hunslet Carr and develop a piece of land owned by the Low Moor Iron and Coal Company. They cleared a mass of rubble, laid a playing surface and erected a stand in time to play their first fixture on 11 February 1888. Hunslet beat Mirfield that day at the new ground, which they had christened Parkside. This photograph is from 1889 and shows the team that played against Dewsbury. From left to right, back row: Groves, Crook, Skirrow, Carr, Kaye, W. Goldthorpe, Summerhill, J. Goldthorpe, Williamson. Middle row: Stevens, Carroll, Gilston, Rathmell, Mosley. Front row: Stephens, Townsend, Lapping, A. Goldthorpe.

Success soon came to Hunslet and by 1892 they had beaten rivals Leeds St John 21-0 in the final of the Yorkshire Cup at Fartown, Huddersfield. In the team were three of the famous Goldthorpe brothers. In all there were five of these brothers who played for Hunslet – William, James, John, Albert and Walter – and the fraternal connection that began in the 1880s with William finally ended in the 1930s when Albert left the football committee. With the famous 'T'owd Tin Pot' are, from left to right, back row: Bennet, J. Goldthorpe, Moore, Skirrow, Groves, W. Goldthorpe. Middle row: Liversedge, A. Goldthorpe, Kay, Lapping, Mosley, Rathmell. Front row: Townend, Gilston, Wright.

Hunslet as depicted on a Baines of Bradford card during the early part of the century. The cards were the forerunner of the modern day collectors' cards and the Hunslet club and players were featured on several of them.

Billy Gilston's enormous popularity and fame led to him be featured on many cards. Here he is depicted around 1890 on a card issued by Richardson of Leeds.

Hunslet's success led to the signing of several well-known players, including Jack Shooter the England Rugby Union international signed from Morley Rugby Union club. Shooter, pictured here with his English team-mates prior to a game against Scotland, is on the far right of the back row.

THE LEADER OF THE HUNSLET PACK.

JACK SHOOTER.

A caricature of Jack Shooter depicting him as leader of the Hunslet pack

Early photographers tended to concentrate on individuals and teams, therefore action shots from early Northern Union games are very rare. This picture was taken at the Boulevard in around 1903/04 and captures an unknown Hunslet defender (in the white shirt) about to tackle a Hull player.

Hunslet, by being beaten on Christmas Day and Boxing Day, have lost their place in the first four in the Northern Rugby League.

The Tyke : This 'ere leuks like ower much Xmas, nah ah'm tellin' yer.

Hunslet depicted as a Christmas pudding having lost games on Christmas Day and Boxing Day, thus slipping out of the top four.

In 1905 the Parksiders collected their first major trophy since joining the Northern Union, becoming the first holders of the Yorkshire Challenge Cup. Hunslet defeated juniors Saville Green, Keighley and Hull Kingston Rovers to meet Halifax in the final at Park Avenue, Bradford. A crowd of 18,500 witnessed a try from Charlie Ward, two goals from Walter Goldthorpe and a hat-trick of goals from Albert Goldthorpe to see Hunslet defeat Halifax 13-3.

The first ever winners of the Yorkshire Cup strike a traditional pose with the trophy. From left to right, back row: Glew, W. Wray, Jukes, Uttley, Hannah, Williamson, Everson, Walsh, Shooter. Middle row: Eagers, Haycox, A. Goldthorpe, W. Goldthorpe, Brookes, Wilson. Front row: Jackson, W. Ward, Place, C. Ward.

Walter Goldthorpe was the youngest of the five brothers. He began his career at Parkside in the 1889/90 season at the age of fifteen. Walter was a pacey centre three-quarter who was a master of the art of kicking the ball across the face of the opposing team's defence. He left Hunslet in 1909, having made over 400 appearances, transferring to Leeds where he collected a Challenge Cup winners medal in 1910.

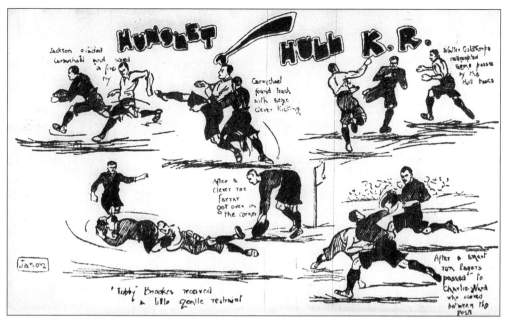

Action sketches from the 1906/07 season as Hunslet take on Hull Kingston Rovers (above) and Halifax (below) at Parkside.

In the early years of the Northern Union Hunslet were famous for their large and powerful forward formations. In December 1909 the club granted a joint benefit to two of their most famous forwards; Harry Wilson and Tommy Walsh had both played in the Challenge Cup final of 1899 when the Parksiders lost 9-19 to Oldham at Manchester. Harry Wilson played just under 450 games for Hunslet in career that lasted fifteen years.

A comic card featuring a young Albert Goldthorpe produced by Baines of Bradford.

The players' individual popularity was soon harnessed by companies to promote their products. Fred Farrar endorsed 'Zam-Buk', praising its use for football–related injuries. Farrar, who was nick-named 'The Farsley Flyer', was signed from Bramley during the 1906/07 season. His speed and direct running enabled him to score many fine tries, including 17 during the 1907/08 season. He transferred to Keighley in 1912 but returned to Hunslet to as a 'guest' player when the rules were relaxed during the emergency leagues of the First World War.

The visit to England and Wales by New Zealand, the first overseas tourists, in 1907/08 saw several Hunslet players honoured with selection for Yorkshire and England. On 18 December 1907 Yorkshire entertained New Zealand at Belle Vue, Wakefield. Harry Wilson (second player from the left on the back row) and Fred Farrar (third from the right on the front row) were members of the side that lost 23-4.

Harry Wilson (third player from the left on the back row) also played for England in the game against New Zealand at Central Park, Wigan.

The first tour to England by Australia saw the Kangaroos visit Hunslet on 7 November 1908. Despite tries by Billy Jukes, Billy Batten and Jack Randall the Parksiders were narrowly beaten 12-11. A series of sketches commissioned for the local newspaper captured the scenes at Parkside.

The Yorkshire team for the game against Lancashire at the Boulevard, Hull, had three Hunslet players: Herbert Place (second player from the left in the middle row), Harry Wilson (with the ball in the middle row) and Fred Smith (in the centre of the front row). Place kicked 2 goals and Smith scored a try to help the Tykes defeat Lancashire 27-14.

"Good Luck! Hunslet."

BY "THE HERMIT."

His Nibs: Ah 'ope ahsall be able ter tak another sup wi' yer in t'owd pot at t'end o' this season, Albert.

'His Nibs', a popular cartoon strip in the local newspapers of the era, is seen wishing Albert Goldthorpe and some of his team-mates good luck at the start of the 1908/09 season.

In 1910 the Northern Union sent its first squad of players to Australia and New Zealand. Hunslet had four players in the touring party: Billy Batten (second from the left in the third row), Billy Jukes (first on the left in the second row), Fred Smith (second from the left in the front row) and Fred Farrar (second from the right in the front row). Billy Batten played in 12 tour games, including all the Test matches, and scored 5 tries and a goal. Fred Smith also played 12 games, including three Tests, and scored 4 tries. Billy Jukes also played 12 games, including all the Tests, and scored 10 tries (including a hat-trick in the first test in Sydney – a record for a forward which still stands today). Fred Farrar was an unlucky tourist as he was hampered by a succession of injuries and made just 4 appearances, scoring 4 tries and a goal.

The Hunslet committee constantly scoured England and (especially) Wales for new players but in January 1912 surprised even their most ardent followers by signing Lucius Banks, a coloured American serviceman. Banks, a twenty-three year old Cavalryman from Arlington Mass., was spotted playing American Football by an Hunslet committeeman and promptly bought out of the army and shipped across to South Leeds. His signing received a mixed reaction in the local press, many regarding his acquisition as merely a crowd-pulling exercise that denied local players the chance to play for Hunslet. Not surprisingly he made little impact on the field and played most of his few games in the reserves. Banks is pictured here with Jukes, Fowler, Randall and Wyburn.

TEAMS AND SCORING SHEET FOR TO-DAY.

No.	HUNSLET	Score Goals	Tries	No.	YORK	Score Goals	Tries
	FULL BACK.				**FULL BACK.**		
1	H. Place	....		1	F. Moore	....	
	THREE-QUARTER BACKS.				**THREE-QUARTER BACKS.**		
2	F. Farrar	....					
3	W. Batten	....		2	J. J. Mills	....	
4	J. Batten	....		3	F. W. Oliver	....	
5	A. Jenkinson	....		4	J. Dillon	....	
10	L. Banks, Jun.	....		5	J. W. Duckworth	......	
	HALF BACKS.				**HALF BACKS.**		
6	F. Smith	....		6	W. Boggin	....	
7	H. Toft	....		7	G. W. Daniel	....	
	FORWARDS.						
8	W. Jukes	....			**FORWARDS.**		
9	H. Wilson	....		8	F. Balmforth	....	
11	J. W. Smales	....		9	L. F. Calvert	....	
12	J. Randall	....		10	H. Conyers	....	
14	J. Wyburn	....		11	H. Havelock	....	
15	W. Fowler	....		12	P. Nickson	....	
16	H. Banks	....		13	G. Lupton	....	

Referee, Mr. R. Robinson (Bradford).
Touch Judges: Messrs. H. G. Roebuck (Huddersfield) and F. W. Tattersall (Wakefield).

The line-up from the official *Parkside Echo* for the Hunslet v. York match, which records the debut of Lucius Banks. Hunslet won the game 28-7 and Banks scored a try in his first game for Hunslet thanks to a pass from Billy Batten.

The Hull and Hunslet teams pose with a trophy awarded to the winners of the games played between the two clubs at the Boulevard, *c.* 1912. Hunslet, in the white shirts, still have some members of their 'four cups' team in the group. From left to right, back row: Billy Batten, Guerin, H. Banks, Jukes, Smith. Middle row: Place, Smales, Mitchell. Front row: James Batten, Jenkinson, Fearn. Directly behind the Hull players are Wyburn (second from the right) and Fowler (fourth from right).

Hull and Hunslet, again at the Boulevard. To the right of the trophy in the middle row is Billy Batten, the Hunslet three-quarter who was later to transfer to Hull for the (then) record fee of £600. Batten, who was one of the great names of the Northern Union, made his debut with Hunslet in 1906/07 and the following year, in his first full season at Parkside, he collected four of his many medals.

In 1914 Great Britain toured Australian and New Zealand for a second time. Jack Smales (second from the right in the back row), Walter Guerin (fourth from the left in the third row) and Fred Smith (second from the right in the front row) were Hunslet's representatives. Jack Smales played 7 games scoring 2 tries. The Lions began the tour in fine style, beating South Australia 101-0 in Adelaide, scoring 23 tries in the process. They played a total of 12 games in Australia, winning 9 and losing just 3. In New Zealand the tourists won all 6 of their games. The players received wages of 10s. a day whilst at sea and £1 a day on land. The tour was a successful one and made profits of over £3,000. Each player received a bonus of £60.

Eddie Guerin, of Hunslet.—One of the giants of the game. Usually gets what he wants—points!

Walter Guerin played in 8 games, scoring a single try and 12 goals.

Fred Smith made 12 appearances on the tour and played in all five Test matches against Australia and New Zealand, including the famous 'Rorkes Drift' Test at Sydney when an injury-ravaged British side held out against all the odds to beat Australia.

Two
All Four Cups

Hunslet's inspirational captain Albert Goldthorpe. He was one of the finest exponents of tactical kicking the game has ever seen – a contemporary newspaper report of his play recorded that 'There was only one man who kicked with judgement and he was Albert Goldthorpe, Hunslet's guide, philosopher, and friend. Generally when he put his foot to the ball it was to the advantage of his side.'

The most successful Hunslet side in the history of the club proudly pose with 'All Four Cups' at the end of the record-breaking 1907/08 season. Hunslet were the first side to win all the four trophies available to them, a feat which was only achieved by two other clubs, Huddersfield and Swinton. The feat is now impossible, since various changes and the advent of Super League have reduced the trophies on display to just one, the Challenge Cup. The players are, from left to right, back row: J.T. Wray, W. Goldthorpe, J. Smales, W. Hannah (trainer), C. Cappleman, J. Randall, W. Jukes. Middle row: W. Wray, C. Ward, W. Ward, A.E. Goldthorpe, W. Batten, H. Place, W. Brookes. J.W. Higson. Front row: W. Hoyle, F. Whittaker, F. Smith, W. Eagers. The trophies are, from left to right: Yorkshire Cup, Yorkshire League Trophy, Challenge Cup, Championship Trophy.

On 26 October 1907, 5,000 attended the Huddersfield *v.* Hunslet league match at Fartown. Hunslet defeated Huddersfield 17-11 thanks to tries from Farrar, Wilson and Batten, 3 goals (including 1 drop goal) from Albert Goldthorpe and a drop goal from Billy Eagers. Cumbrian Eagers was an enigmatic character who delighted in the unexpected. A journalist once wrote of him 'Eagers is a law unto himself, he exasperated one by doing the most absurd things, yet a moment after one of the eccentricities he will score a fine try. Eagers is the despair of the orthodox, but he is very valuable to Hunslet.'

An artist's impression of the game at Bradford on 16 November 1907. The game was played at Grenfield Stadium, Dudley Hill, Bradford's home for just one season. Hunslet won the match 9-6 thanks to a try from Billy Batten, 2 goals from Albert Goldthorpe and a drop goal from Herbert Place.

Hunslet collected their first of their four trophies on 21 December, beating holders Halifax in the Yorkshire Cup final at Headingley, Leeds. They had defeated Bramley 50-0, local rivals Leeds 17-10 and Wakefield Trinity 10-0 to reach the final for the second time in three years. The Parksiders' great forwards dominated the play in the final, winning possession in five out of every six scrums and paved the way for Hunslet's 17-0 victory. Albert Goldthorpe scored a try, a goal and a drop goal, Smith and Batten scored tries and C. Ward and Eagers dropped goals. From left to right, back row: Smales, Farrar, Higson, Hannah (trainer), Wilson, W. Wray, Cappleman, Middle row: Eagers, Randall, W. Ward, A. Goldthorpe, Jukes, Brookes, W. Goldthorpe. Front row: C. Ward, Place, Smith, Batten, Walsh.

Billy Hannah was Hunslet's 'man with the magic sponge'. A Cumbrian by birth, Hannah had played for Hunslet in the early part of the century and was renowned as a sprinter who could score spectacular tries. He believed that his players should hold down full employment away from the football field and the more physically demanding the job the better the player.

Hunslet met Leeds on four occasions during the 'All Four Cups' season of 1907/08, completing a League double and knocking the Lioners out of the Yorkshire and Challenge Cup competitions. The first round of the Challenge Cup match at Headingley was a stormy affair that saw Hunslet triumph 14-5 and Wade of Leeds and Batten of Hunslet sent off for fighting.

Fred Smith played in 42 games during the 1907/08 season, scoring 17 tries. Born in Woodlesford, he had played Association Football for Kippax before joining Hunslet in 1906. Often overshadowed by his half-back partner, Albert Goldthorpe, Smith was once described as 'one of the sturdiest and strongest halves in the game'.

The Hunslet committee line up in front of the cricket pavilion at Parkside. Second from the right in the middle row is Albert Goldthorpe.

Hunslet's incredible feat of winning everything available to them was in many ways due the form of their forwards. As the season progressed, Lancashire clubs who opposed the Hunslet pack of forwards dubbed them 'The Terrible Six'. The name stuck and has become part of the folklore of both the Hunslet club and the game itself. John Willie Higson, one of the six, had joined the Parksiders from Featherstone Rovers in 1905/06.

Higson was later transferred to Huddersfield where, remarkably, he once again collected all four cups in a single season.

35

Oldham Lose at Hunslet.

Place fielded well

Thomas underwent a gruelling at the start.

Avery got Oldham's first try.

Hunslet's first try was obtained by Wilson.

White initiated a fine movement which ended in Llewellyn scoring.

Brookes made his mark.

An artist's impression of the Challenge Cup second round match against Oldham at Parkside. For the first time in the season Hunslet were missing their captain, Albert Goldthorpe, who was suffering from 'runner's breakdown', but still defeated Oldham 15-8 before a crowd of 20,000. Once again 'The Terrible Six' were awesome and Flaneur of the local paper wrote of them, 'The staying power of the Hunslet forwards is little short of marvellous. For 80 minutes they were going at top pressure, yet their last rush was as vigorous and dangerous as their first'.

Bill 'Tubby' Brookes was a giant 14st 10lb forward who joined Hunslet from Kippax in 1900/01.

When Batten's idea ... such a Hunslet germinates, one wonders if "Tubby" Brookes will turn out to honour his old club.

A caricature of 'Tubby' Brookes contemplating playing in a benefit game at Parkside long after his retirement

Jack Randall was another one of the famous forwards. He was signed from Featherstone Rovers in 1906/07.

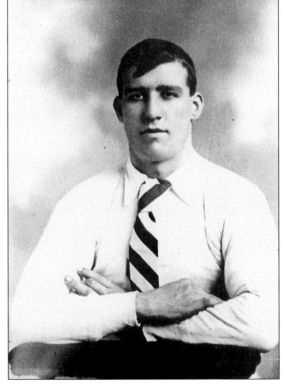

John 'Jack' Smales, another member of 'The Terrible Six', who signed from Outwood Church in 1906. A contemporary match report of a Hunslet game in which the forwards were at their peak commented, 'Their stamina, their perfect cohesion and above all, their playing intelligence, has to be seen to be thoroughly appreciated'.

The defeat of Broughton Rangers, the crack Manchester-based side, in the Championship semi-final was one of the Parksiders' finest victories of the season. The 28-3 rout was due, once again, to the tremendous form of the Hunslet pack of forwards

Harry Wilson was a thirty year old veteran forward who had played Rugby Union for Methley, Castleford, Rothwell, Morley and Yorkshire before joining Hunslet in the 1898/99 season.

Tom Walsh was the brother of Owen – an early Hunslet stalwart. Tom joined Hunslet in 1896/97 and was a policeman by profession.

A contemporary sketch of the drawn Championship final at Salford. Hunslet won the replay 12-2 at Belle Vue, Wakefield to collect their record-breaking fourth trophy of the season.

Portraits of Hunslet's 1907/08 squad arranged with the four trophies.

Hunslet's May queens proudly pose with all four cups in the stand at the Parkside ground.

The trophies were the central part of the annual May pageant and were paraded through the streets on a cart drawn by a well turned out dray horse.

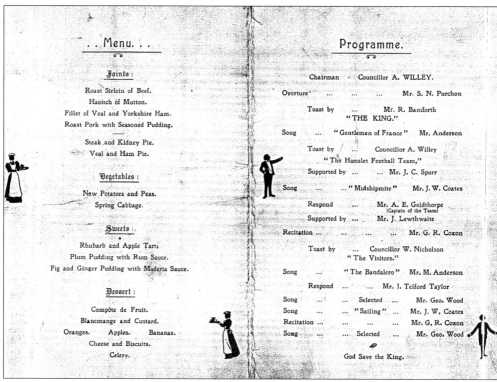

.. Menu. . .

Joints :

Roast Sirloin of Beef.
Haunch of Mutton.
Fillet of Veal and Yorkshire Ham.
Roast Pork with Seasoned Pudding.

Steak and Kidney Pie.
Veal and Ham Pie.

Vegetables :

New Potatoes and Peas.
Spring Cabbage.

Sweets :

Rhubarb and Apple Tart.
Plum Pudding with Rum Sauce.
Fig and Ginger Pudding with Maderia Sauce.

Dessert :

Compôte de Fruit.
Blancmange and Custard.
Oranges.   Apples.   Bananas.
Cheese and Biscuits.
Celery.

Programme.

Chairman - Councillor A. WILLEY.		
Overture	Mr. S. N. Purchon	
Toast by ...	Mr. R. Bamforth	
"THE KING."		
Song ... "Gentlemen of France"	Mr. Anderson	
Toast by ...	Councillor A. Willey	
"The Hunslet Football Team,"		
Supported by	Mr. J. C. Spurr	
Song ... ..."Midshipmite"	Mr. J. W. Coates	
Respond ...	Mr. A. E. Goldthorpe	
(Captain of the Team)		
Supported by ...	Mr. J. Lewthwaite	
Recitation	Mr. G. R. Coxon	
Toast by ...	Councillor W. Nicholson	
"The Visitors."		
Song ...	"The Bandalero"	Mr. M. Anderson
Respond	Mr. J. Telford Taylor	
Song ...	Selected ...	Mr. Geo. Wood
Song ...	... "Sailing" ...	Mr. J. W. Coates
Recitation ...		Mr. G. R. Coxon
Song ...	... Selected ...	Mr. Geo. Wood

God Save the King.

The menu and programme for a celebration dinner given in Hunslet.

The four trophies were displayed throughout Hunslet including shop windows.

Three
Between the Wars

A caricature of Jack Walkington on a cigarette card of the era.

Hunslet in 1924/25. From left to right, back row: Tegardine, Crowther, Sage, Bennett, Moss, Clarkson. Middle row: Jones, Dawson, Guerin, Coulson, Stockwell. Front row: Young, Cottam. Hooker Charles Sage was capped twice by Wales in 1925, opposing England on both occasions at Workington and Wigan. The season was a average one for the Parksiders, they finished thirteenth in the league table with 19 victories and 17 defeats.

Place, Coulson and Nicholson pose outside the dressing rooms at Thrum Hall, Halifax in January 1928.

Ernest Young, a popular half-back during the lean years of the 1920s, poses in his Yorkshire County cap. Young played in the Yorkshire v. Lancashire game at Thrum Hall, Halifax in November 1924.

Litts, Dai Jenkins and Les White in 1928. Prop forward Jenkins was capped three times by Wales while he was with Hunslet. He joined Leeds in 1932.

Broughton, Beverley, Guerin and Walkington at Thrum Hall. Harry Beverley, a clever, ball-handling forward, was once described as constructive rather than destructive. He played Association Football, gaining honours with Leeds schoolboys, before taking up Rugby League in 1926. Beverley joined Hunslet in 1928/29 season as a centre and left Parkside to join Halifax in 1937.

Hector Crowther, Ernest Young and Frank 'Dolly' Dawson in 1928. Hector Crowther played several times for Yorkshire and opposed the Australians for Great Britain in the famous fourth Test at Rochdale on 15 January 1930. He made a total of 467 appearances for Hunslet in a career that spanned fifteen years.

Walter 'Eddie' Guerin was a six foot, sixteen stone giant signed in 1911 from Hartlepool Rugby Union Club. Geurin made an instant impact at Parkside, scoring a try and goal on his debut against Bramley. He went on to score over 1,100 points in just over 350 games in a remarkable career that stretched until 1928.

Leslie White was signed from Pontypridd Rugby League Club in 1928. A hugely competitive hooker he was capped 7 times for Wales and toured Australia with the 1932 British Lions. By the time he retired in 1946 Les had made 493 appearances for the club.

White is in the very centre of the back row of this tour photograph taken at the famous Sydney Cricket Ground. He played in 9 games, including four Test matches against both Australia and New Zealand, and scored 3 tries.

Hector Crowther was one of Hunslet's finest second row forwards during the 1920s and early 1930s. He signed for Hunslet in 1918 and in later years forged a famous partnership with Frank Dawson, the pair playing a huge part in the 1934 Challenge Cup campaign.

Frank 'Dolly' Dawson was a fiery, teak-tough forward in the great traditions of 'The Terrible Six'. He signed for Hunslet in 1921/22 as a centre and learned his rugby craft there before moving to the thick of the action in the forwards. 'Dolly' played his last season at Parkside in 1937/38, retiring after the game against Batley on 23 October 1937.

In 1927/28 Parkside hosted the Yorkshire *v.* Glamorgan and Monmouthshire County Championship game. Yorkshire, with Hunslet's Walkington, Broughton and Crowther in their ranks, defeated the Welsh side 20-12. Surrounded by many of the Parkside crowd, Glamorgan and Monmouthshire are, from left to right, standing: Davies, Gore, Brown, Sullivan, Coles, Green. Seated: Thompson, Lewis, Flynn, Fairfax, Ring, Parker. Front: Andrews.

Jack Walkington, only the second ever Hunslet player to collect both Challenge Cup and Championship Trophy. Walkington signed for Hunslet in 1927 from Burley Rugby Union Club for the then astounding sum of £300. He soon became an accomplished centre, scoring a pair of tries and a goal on his debut for the club. After three seasons at centre he dropped back to fill the specialist full-back role with great success. He was a natural goal-kicker and during his career kicked 577 goals in 572 games. Jack retired in 1948 to concentrate on his successful cabinet-making business in Bramley.

On the far right of this quartet of Hunslet players is Harold Buck, one of the fastest wing men of his generation. A talented association footballer before joining Hunslet, Buck was the subject of the first £1,000 transfer when he left Parkside to join Leeds in November 1921. He achieved great success at Headingley, collecting a Challenge Cup winners medal in 1923 before returning to end his playing days at Parkside.

William 'Billy' Thornton learned his Rugby League football with Hunslet Carr schoolboys and played in side that was unbeaten in three seasons and once scored 145 points in 55 minutes. Perhaps bored with his success, Thornton took up soccer but returned to his first love in 1927 when he signed for Hunslet. He started life as a stand-off but switched to scrum-half in 1929 to form a brilliant partnership with George Todd. He retired in 1946 having amassed 431 games for the club.

A muddied but still smiling Hunslet side in 1932/33, when they finished the season in seventh place having won 23 games and lost 15. From left to right: Crowther, White, Smith, Tolson, Dennis, Riach, Thornton, Walkington, Morrell, Winter, Dawson, Goulthorpe and Broughton.

Following the Challenge Cup final victory of 1934 the club embarked on a short tour of France to help establish the newly-formed French Rugby League. They played their first game at Bordeaux where they were surprisingly beaten 38-23. Four days later the Hunslet party were in Pau where they recovered some pride and defeated the local side 33-19.

Hunslet in 1934/35. From left to right, back row: Plenderleith, Dawson, Tolson, Smith, White, Beverley, Grainge. Front row: Yates, Walkington, Todd, Thornton, Dennis, Winter. The season was far from successful for Hunslet, who finished in eleventh place. However, it represented a personal triumph for George Dennis who established the club's try-scoring record. On 20 January Hunslet trounced Bradford Northern 57-2 at Parkside and Dennis bettered George Todd's six tries in a match record (set the previous season) by crossing for seven – a record that still stands today. A match report of the game from a local newspaper said of Dennis, 'He showed speed and determination in going for the line against an opponent much bigger and stronger in the person of Pilling, secured by Bradford a few days before from Wigan'.

Eric Batten was plucked from the relative obscurity of the Wakefield Trinity reserve team in 1936 by a shrewd Hunslet scout. The signing was a great one for Batten – son of the famous Billy who played for Hunslet in 1907/08 – and the club as he helped the Parksiders to the Championship in 1938 and became one of the finest wing men of the era.

Just as they had in 1934, Hunslet visited France for a short tour following the Championship victory of 1938. Several of the players and committee are pictured here posing at Marseilles harbour at the start of the tour.

Action from a game in France in 1938.

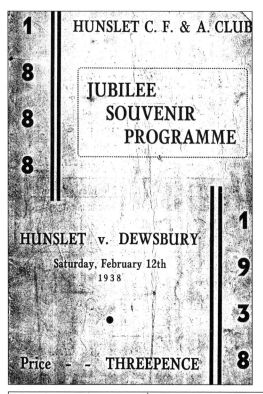

HUNSLET C. F. & A. CLUB

1888

JUBILEE SOUVENIR PROGRAMME

HUNSLET v. DEWSBURY

Saturday, February 12th
1938

1938

Price - - THREEPENCE

In 1938 Hunslet celebrated fifty years at their Parkside ground with a jubilee match against Dewsbury. Among the many speeches given were ones by Billy Gilston and Albert Goldthorpe. A special souvenir programme was produced for the match, which Hunslet won.

The line up for the Hunslet v. Dewsbury Jubilee match taken from the official programme.

Oliver John Morris was signed in 1937 from Pontypridd Rugby Union Club and within weeks was capped by Wales. Slightly-built, Morris hardly looked the saviour he was to become. On the field of play his lightening cut through, 'quick Welsh hands' and tenacious tackling more than compensated for his diminutive frame. Morris made his debut against Newcastle on 20 November 1937. His electric performances at Parkside soon caught the eyes of the selectors and he played 3 times against the English and twice against France. He is on the far right front row of this group of Welsh players and officials pictured outside their hotel in Bordeaux following an international with France.

Hunslet were drawn against Liverpool Stanley in the first round of the 1938 Challenge Cup competition. The LMS railway ran a special excursion train but the Parksiders Cup dreams of the twin towers of Wembley ended on the west coast, Liverpool beating them 6-5.

The Hunslet team and officials line up for a game during their short tour of France.

Four

Wembley '34

NORTH
GRAND
STAND

Reserved Seat
(Unnumbered)

ENTER AT TURNSTILES
(See Plan on back)

F

ENTRANCE **77**

Empire Stadium, Wembley

RUGBY LEAGUE FINAL

Saturday, May 5th, 1934

(Kick-off 3.0 p.m.)

Price 3/–
(Including Tax)

A. J. Elvin

MANAGING DIRECTOR,
Wembley Stadium Limited.

THIS PORTION TO BE RETAINED
(See Conditions on back)

A rare collectors item in the shape of a ticket for the final, which cost three shillings including tax.

The cover for the 1934 Challenge Cup final between Hunslet and Widnes. The Parksiders, despite playing much of the game with a man short, were worthy 11-5 victors over the local thirteen of Widnes.

Twelve of Hunslet's thirteen players for the semi-final against Huddersfield line up for the pre-match photographs at Wakefield's Belle Vue ground. The Parksiders had beaten Leigh, Castleford, and York in the rounds leading to the semi-final. At Wakefield it was the craft and hard work of Thornton and Todd and the defence-splitting runs of Jack Walkington that had paved the way for the 12-7 victory.

A photograph of Hunslet players and committeemen was presented free with the *Daily Despatch* on the morning of the final.

The Hunslet team are introduced to Lord Derby before the Wembley final. Leaning forward to shake hands is Cyril Morrell, a former Hunslet Carr schoolboy who joined the Parksiders in 1931 as a half-back. At the beginning of the 1933/34 season he switched positions to play in the centre. It was Morrell who scored Hunslet's first try at Wembley when, in the 26th minute, he latched on to a brilliant pass from Winter to sprint over the line for a crucial but costly score. In the very act of scoring Morrell broke his collar bone and although he attempted to play on had to leave the field. Without the modern day luxury of a substitute the Parksiders were reduced to twelve men for the rest of the game.

Despite the loss of their centre, Hunslet stuck to their task and produced one of the finest and bravest displays seen under the famous twin towers of the Empire Stadium. The veteran Crowther and Dawson played a major part in Hunslet's victory, *The Yorkshire Post* commenting that, 'These two grand old forwards have served Hunslet well for many years, but never better than at the scene of Hunslet's greatest triumph today.'

'Dolly' Dawson plunges in to the Widnes defence in a typical barnstorming run.

Prop forward Len Smith races forward in an attempt to gather a loose ball. Smith was a gifted schoolboy footballer who gained honours with the Leeds City schools sides in the mid-1920s. He joined the Parksiders in 1928 and one of the highlights of his career came when he scored Hunslet's third try at Wembley.

Billy Thornton, the gifted half-back whose clever tactics were a major part in Hunslet's victory.

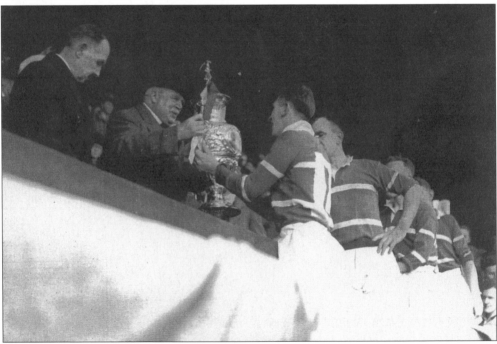

Jack Walkington pauses for a few words with Lord Derby as he becomes only the second Hunslet captain to collect the Challenge Cup.

The joyful players parade the cup in front of the thousands of fans who had travelled down to London for the final. The players are, from left to right: Todd, Winter, Tolson, Thornton, Dawson, Walkington (with the cup), Beverley, Smith, Crowther and Dennis.

Jack Walkington (with the Challenge Cup) and his happy players continue their celebrations as they leave their London hotel for the rail journey back to Yorkshire.

Dolly Dawson and the club's physiotherapist with the Challenge Cup in front of the Hunslet cricket pavilion.

Back at their Parkside base, the Hunslet team pose for an official photograph with the Challenge Cup. From left to right, back row: Crowther, Dawson, Tolson, Beverley, Smith, Whitehead, White. Middle row: Lewthwaite, Dennis, Morrell, Walkington, Winter, Broughton, Hannah. Front row: Todd, Thornton. For Lewthwaite and Hannah it was the second time they had posed with the Challenge Cup as both were involved with Hunslet when they won all four cups in 1908.

Five
The All Leeds Final

Official Souvenir Programme

NORTHERN RUGBY LEAGUE
CHAMPIONSHIP
FINAL GAME

HUNSLET
v. LEEDS

Played at ELLAND ROAD
(Ground of LEEDS UNITED A.F.C.)

Saturday, April 30th, 1938

Kick-off 3-30 p.m.

Price . . . . . . Threepence

The cover of the programme for 1938 Championship final between Hunslet and Leeds. The game, which was played at Elland Road, the home of Leeds United, was the first meeting in a major final of the two cross-city rivals since the Rugby Union Yorkshire Cup final of 1892 and once again it was the south side of the river that triumphed, Hunslet collecting the trophy with an 8-2 victory.

Colin Stansfield shakes hands before the kick-off. Originally planned for Belle Vue, Wakefield the game was switched to Leeds following a wave of protests from both clubs, newspapers and scores of fans eager to see the 'All Leeds Final' played in Leeds.

Hunslet's Irish wingman O'Sullivan turns to pass just as he is tackled by a Leeds player. O'Sullivan put Hunslet into a commanding position with a well-taken try after 30 minutes of play. The huge crowd forming a dramatic backdrop to the scene was 54,112 – a new world record for a Rugby League game.

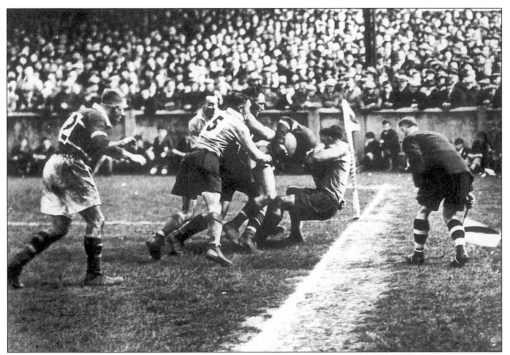

Eric Batten is bundled into touch by a posse of Leeds defenders as Colin Stansfield rushes across to assist his colleague.

Cyril Morrell halts a Leeds attack with a superb head-on tackle. The Parksiders' fine defence weathered a torrid twenty-minute opening spell from the speedy Leeds backs before Winter opened the Hunslet scoring with a brilliant try in the 23rd minute.

Eric Batten leaves a pair of Hull defenders in despair as he cruises over the line for another superb try. Batten was Hunslet's top scorer during the 1937/38 league campaign with 30 tries from 31 appearances.

Sam Newbound was one of the youngest members of the Hunslet squad for the final. He was a keen body-builder, winning several medals for his athletic build.

Eric Harris, the Loiners' Australian wingman, tackles Eric Batten.

Australian Vic Hey, the Leeds half-back, holds the Championship trophy as he shakes hands with Hunslet's victorious captain Jack Walkington. In between the two rival captains stands Jim Lewthwaite, the Hunslet chairman.

A bruised and battered Jack Walkington poses with the Championship Trophy in the dressing rooms of Elland Road.

Back at their Parkside home the players and committee gather in front of the Hunslet Cricket
Club pavilion for an official photograph. From left to right (players only), back row: Newbound,
Tolson, Bennett, Stansfield. Middle row: White, Morrell, Thornton, Walkington, Plenderleith,
O'Sullivan, Thompson. Front row: Batten, Morris. Inserts: Winter, Tiffany, Yates.

Sam Newbound, Eddie Bennett, Mark Tolson, Cyril Plenderleith, Les White, Billy Thornton
and Cyril Morrell with the Championship Trophy.

Hunslet's Championship season ended with a well-earned benefit match for their captain Jack Walkington. The two sides are all smiles as they mix before the kick-off at Parkside. Walkington shakes hands with Huddersfield's Alex Fiddes, his opposing captain for the game.

The Parkside faithful are treated to a look at the Championship Trophy as Jack Walkington proudly displays the cup before his benefit match.

Six

Derby Days

FLOODLIT RUGBY LEAGUE GAME

HUNSLET v. LEEDS

ELLAND ROAD, LEEDS

(By courtesy of the Directors of Leeds United A.F.C. Ltd.)

MONDAY, SEPTEMBER 29th, 1958, kick-off 7.30 p.m.

Programme . . . Threepence

CLUB NOTES.

To-day brings back vivid memories of that memorable match on Saturday, April 30th, 1938, HUNSLET v LEEDS in the final for the League Championship. Hunslet had finished in the top position of the league table and Leeds were second. Both clubs won their semi-finals, defeating Barrow and Swinton respectively. By the courtesy of the Leeds United Directors, who delayed their Central League fixture to Saturday evening, this final was played at Elland Road and commenced the fashion of playing future league finals on capacious soccer grounds.

Anticipation of a huge crowd was exceeded by events, un-precedented in the annals of our game. The gates were closed leaving thousands outside who were naturally very disappointed. A remarkable attendance of 54,112 were crowded into the ground and after a thrilling game Hunslet came out the winners by 8 points to 2.

Again by the courtesy of the Leeds United Directors we are privileged to stage this local "Derby" on their fine ground with its modern amenities. It has often been said that bitter enmity exists between those who support the respective codes, Rugby and Soccer. We would agree that there is great rivalry but nevertheless, there exists a great friendship between Hunslet and Leeds United just as there is between Hunslet and Leeds. Of course when we are playing our local rivals from Headingley no quarter is asked for or given on either side. The will to win is the paramount factor but not at any price. "Dogfights" which occasionally took place in the "good old days" we want to see no more, and for many, many seasons now the games between our two clubs have been a delight to watch.

In late September 1958 Hunslet met Leeds under floodlghts at Elland Road. Just as they had done twenty years earlier Hunslet defeated Leeds 15-8.

The early derby matches between Hunslet and Leeds attracted tremendous interest in the city and the local newspapers did much to report and publicise the games. This is an artist's impression of the Hunslet *v.* Leeds league game at Parkside on 6 October 1905. Despite a try from Charlie Ward the Parksiders were trounced 17-5 by their rivals from Headingley.

The same game captured by the resident artist from a rival newspaper.

The Hunslet *v.* Leeds match at Parkside on 3 October 1908 was captured superbly by a local artist. The Parksiders defeated the Loiners 13-10 in a hard fought game that typified the derby matches.

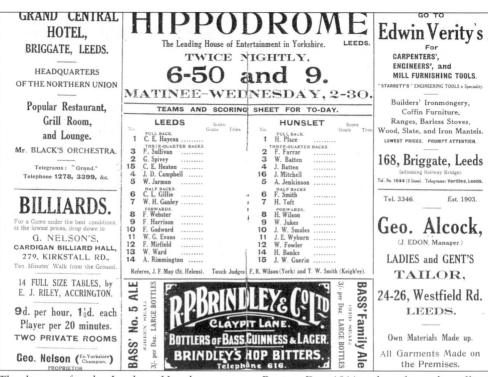

The line-up for the Leeds v. Hunslet game on Boxing Day 1911, taken from the official programme. Billy Batten is partnered by his brother James and several of the 'All Four Cups' squad are still present for the Parksiders.

In 1911, Mr Lazenby, a member of the Leeds committee, presented a silver cup for annual competition between Leeds and Hunslet. The aim was to establish a fund to provide playing fields for teams in the Leeds junior leagues. Leeds were the first holders but lost 11-9 in August 1930, when this photograph of the Hunslet team at Headingley was taken. From left to right, back row: Chapman, White, Crowther, D.M. Jenkins, Dawson, Traill, Beverley. Front row: Walkington, Adams, Bell, Todd, Thornton, Broughton.

Billy Thornton roars with delight as he beats a Leeds defender during a derby game at Headingley. A huge crowd and the steeple of the famous St Michaels church provides a superb backdrop to this photograph.

The Parksider

Official Guide and Programme of the Hunslet Rugby Football Club

Saturday, October 5th, 1940

PRESIDENT—Sir Wm. NICHOLSON
COMMITTEE—Football Section :
VICE-PRESIDENTS—Messrs. J. Lewthwaite (Chairman) E. Meeks (Vice-Chairman)
W. Waide
COMMITTEE—Messrs. J. C. Barwick, W. Chadwick, T. Cooper, G. Farrar,
A. Kennedy, S. Lees, G. W. Lightfoot, Dr. P. Pollard, G. C. Richardson, H. Whiteley

To-day's Teams

HUNSLET

1
Walkington

2		3		4		5
Batten		Morrell		Rookes		Turton

6
Booth

7
Watson

8		9		10
Thompson		White		Bennett

11		12		14
Casewell		Burnell		Whitehead

Referee—J. E. Taylor (Wakefield)   Touch Judges—Messrs. E. Flower, B. Laughlin

13		12		11
Cautheray		Foreman		Dyer		Jubb

10		9		8
Phillips		Maskill		Murphy		Baldwin

7
Jenkins

6
Morris

5		4		3		2
Eastwood or F. Harris		Hey		Risman		Toothill

1
Eaton

LEEDS

CLUB CHAT

We ask all our members and supporters to bear with us during prevailing conditions, in issuing a single sheet programme. What space is available we will endeavour to keep you informed of the club's doings. The team has made a splendid start, and there is no reason why our record should not be kept at a high level. Good football worthy of your patronage is our ambition. Your support is necessary to keep the flag flying at Parkside. We know you will do that. Of last year's first team, M. Tolson is a Military Policeman and J. Booth a gunner in the Anti-Aircraft. Also in the Services are Grace, Stansfield and Batchelor. Leeds to-day ! A warm welcome to you, and the hope of a good game.

NOTICE

When an air-raid warning is sounded the match will be suspended until the "Raiders passed" is sounded. Spectators are advised to take refuge under the stands or in any other shelter available on the ground. Spectators are advised not to leave the ground to seek shelter elsewhere, although anyone is at liberty to go home. The match will be abandoned if the warning occurs shortly before the end.

Fred Inman & Son, Ltd., 65, Waterloo Road, Hunslet, Leeds, 10.

A single sheet issue of *The Parksider* for the Hunslet *v.* Leeds match in October 1940. The sheet gives details of what steps to take should an air-raid warning sound during the game. Playing for Leeds at stand-off was Oliver John Morris, a Welshman who had begun his Rugby League career with Hunslet in 1938. A ferociously competitive player, Morris was transferred to Leeds in 1939 with a contract that contained a war clause of a reduction in fee if Europe was at war on a certain date.

Leeds and Hunslet derby action from the 1930s as Leeds players Stan Brogden and Eric Harris work a scissors movement at Parkside

Scenes from the Leeds *v*. Hunslet Challenge Cup match at Headingley in 1947 show a heavy, muddy ground that still has remnants of the straw that was used to protect the pitch from overnight frost. A packed scoreboard end witness a galloping charge from Arthur Clues.

Despite a brilliant tackle from Hunslet's Freddie Williamson, the ball has been passed to Dickie Williams, the diminutive Welsh half-back who was to end his career with Hunslet.

The derby games were often torrid affairs and were actually nick-named 'The dog-fights' in the early days. Freddie Williamson, the Hunslet wingman, grimaces in pain after being stretchered off for touchline attention at Headingley. It was later found that Williamson had in fact broken several ribs.

Al 'Ginger' Burnell bursts clear from a scrum at Parkside with Williamson in support. Behind the play Granville James look on unawares that the scrum has failed to break up and has erupted into a brief but ugly brawl.

The last gasp attempts of Welshmen Griffiths and Williams can do little to stop Verrankamp, the Leeds wingman, scoring at Parkside.

A similar attempt at Leeds also ends in failure as Freddie Williamson evades the clutches of Leeds' Bert Cook to score in the corner at Headingley

It takes four Leeds defenders to stop a young Geoff Gunney at a packed Parkside in an early 1950s derby game.

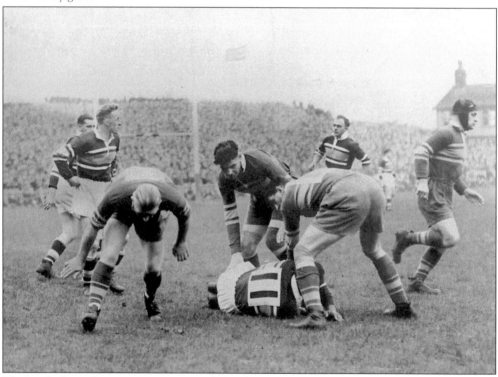

The Leeds players begin to move away and Hunslet start to regroup for another attack. Ted Carroll has taken up the acting half-back position and Fred Burnell comes running to help him.

Leeds forward Arthur Clues flies over the line with Hunslet's Welsh full-back Jack Evans almost upon him. Australian Clues had a seven year career with Leeds before moving across the river to end his playing days with Hunslet

Derby match action at Parkside as Des Clarkson hoists a powerful kick before a trio of advancing Leeds players can reach him. Arthur Clues is the Leeds player on the far right. In later years, both players would change their allegiances, Clarkson joining Leeds in 1949 and Clues moving across the city to Hunslet.

A superb caricature of 'big A' – as Arthur Clues became affectionate known during his Rugby League career in England.

Seven

The Forties and Fifties

A series of caricatures featuring some of the Hunslet players and officials from the mid-fifties.

Following a successful career with Leeds, Australian half-back Vic Hey moved across the river Aire for a brief stint with Hunslet. He was a popular man with both players and supporters and is seen here signing autographs before his return to Australia.

Action at Parkside as Hunslet take on Wakefield Trinity. The winding gear of Middleton Colliery forms a dramatic backdrop to the ground. The stand on the right was originally built in 1913 and closed for a month within three years as workings from the pit caused the foundations to subside.

Three members of the 1934 Challenge Cup final team were in the line-up for the Challenge Cup match between Hunslet and Dewsbury in February 1946. From left to right, back row: Clarkson, Newbound, White, Walkington, Watson, Whitehead, Billings. Front row: Plenderleith, Rookes, Morrell, Williamson, Buck, Ruston.

A Hunslet team from 1947. From left to right, back row: Carroll, Graham, Newbound, Gronow, W. Burnell, Watson, Metcalfe, Goddard. Front row: Williamson, Robinson, Griffiths, Bennett, Ruston.

The 1947/48 season was a reasonably successful one for the Parksiders. In the league they finished in sixth place, winning 21, drawing 4 and losing 11 games, scoring 449 points and conceding 239. From left to right, back row: Clarkson, Bennett, W. Burnell, Metcalfe, Britton, Newbound. Front row: Williamson, A. Burnell, Watson, Graham, Griffiths, Russell, Carroll.

Sid Rookes joined Hunslet after a successful time with the Hunslet National and Yorkshire Schoolboy's teams. Versatile and willing to play anywhere for Hunslet, he appeared as wing, centre, second row and loose forward during his time at Parkside.

Joe Britton, a feriously competitive hooker, pictured in March 1948.

The 1946 Challenge Cup semi-final against Wakefield at Headingley was an epic game for the Parksiders. Billy O'Neil is pictured racing towards the Wakefield try-line. O'Neil had a try disallowed during the game – which Hunslet lost – provoking one disgruntled spectator to leap over the perimeter fence and knock the touch judge out.

Williamson, Traill and Thornton move forward to pressurise the Wakefield defences in the 1946 semi-final.

Ted Carroll was one of Hunslet's finest players during the 1940s and '50s. He retired to become a pub landlord and later took up acting, appearing in several films including a part as a grumpy cobbler in *The Railway Children*.

Hunslet finished a ceditable seventh in the League table in the 1950/51 season, winning 22 of their 36 games. From left to right, back row: Snowden, W. Burnell, Metcalfe, Jones, Harter, Evans, James. Front row: A. Burnell, Artson, Williams, Ormonrovd, Rees, Williamson.

Following retirement from the game, Hunslet's famous Welsh hooker Les White joined the committee and was invaluable at welcoming the many Welsh players Hunslet signed. Relaxing on the famous Parkside wooden perimeter fence, White shows new recruit from the valleys Jack Evans his new club's ground.

A quartet of Welshmen in 1948, from left to right: Jack Evans, Fred Davies, Johnny Russell and Tuss Griffiths.

Before the league match at Fartown on 31 January 1948 the Hunslet and Huddersfield players stood for a minute's silence in memory of Billy Hannah, the former player and coach of the Parksiders.

The Hunslet secretary George Richardson checks the players on board the coach for the Challenge Cup tie against Widnes at Naughton Park.

The Hunslet line-up in February 1948. From left to right, back row: Clarkson, Britton, Metcalfe, Bennett, Newbound, Gronow, Carroll. Front row: Graham, Russell, Burnell, Griffiths, Rookes, Watson. Hunslet won the match 3-0 and went on to face Bradford Northern in the semi-final at Headingley.

The Hunslet cover stream across the Headingley pitch in an attempt to halt the progress of Bradford's Trevor Foster in the 1948 Challenge Cup semi-final match.

Just like his father Jim, Ken Traill began his career with Hunslet before moving to Bradford Northern. Ken's superb side-step and body swerve is captured here as he wrong-foots Fred Williamson and Des Clarkson at Headingley in 1948.

A well-designed programme cover for Hunslet's visit to now-defunct Belle Vue Rangers in late February 1950.

Belle Vue Rangers
(Broughton Rangers
[Belle Vue] Limited)

Telephone:
EASt 1331

2nd ROUND RUGBY LEAGUE CHALLENGE CUP

BELLE VUE RANGERS
v.
HUNSLET

Saturday, February 25th, 1950   Kick-off 3-0 p.m.

Directors :   Alderman W. H. Oldfield, J.P., M.P., J. Kay, and T. Spedding
Secretary-Manager: T. Spedding

TO-DAY'S CUP-TIE

Inter-country rivalry was evenly balanced at the draw for the second round of the Challenge Cup in Manchester on February 13. Four times were Lancashire and Yorkshire clubs paired, and each county stages two of the ties to-day. Leeds and Batley are at home to Wigan and Widnes respectively, while in Lancashire Barrow have Featherstone Rovers as visitors and we entertain Hunslet, to whom we extend a cordial welcome.

As Belle Vue and Hunslet have not had a league fixture this season or last, there are no recent results as a guide to the outcome of to-day's game. Still, how often has it been shown in the past that cup-ties have a habit of producing a result contrary to league form! The last meeting was on April 10, 1948, at Belle Vue, Hunslet winning by a single point (10-9), and in the same season Rangers won at Parkside by 4 points to 2.

Hunslet had an easy task in the first round, meeting the Wigan junior club, Worsley Boys, who they beat by an aggregate score of 63-16. In last

[continued overleaf]

WHITE CHIEF

It's a
TIP TOP LOAF

A PRODUCT OF THE TIP TOP BAKERIES MANCHESTER 18

Official Programme   **Price 2d.**

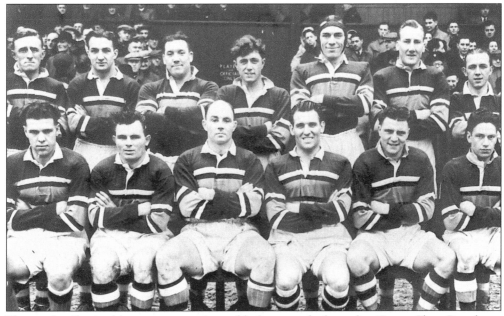

Plenty of smiles in this team group, pictured before a packed stand at Crown Flatt, Dewsbury. From left to right, back row: Carroll, Griffiths, Newbound, James, Metcalfe, Bowman, Talbot. Front row: James, Evans, Jones, Rees, Anson, Potter.

In common with many clubs, Hunslet looked to Australia for players and signed Don Graham. Graham is pictured here running across the face of Huddersfield's Lionel Cooper and flicking a clever pass to his wingman Freddie Williamson.

Training at Parkside, Don Graham leaps from the clutches of a would-be tackler.

Fiercely competitive, Sam Newbound played for Hunslet before and after the Second World War and could be said to be the forerunner of today's 'impact player'. He is shown here clearing the line against Castleford at Parkside with a charging run.

Adept at defence as well as attack, Sam, his face a study of concentration, executes a classic tackle.

Freddie WILLIAMSON

HUNSLET & YORKSHIRE

Freddie Williamson was one of the finest defensive wing men in the game. He played Rugby League with the Hunslet schoolboys but then joined Morley Rugby Union Club at the age of fourteen. He soon graduated to the first XV but luckily for Hunslet and Rugby League football he joined Hunslet in 1943 at the age of twenty.

Another fine try for Williamson as he grounds the ball at his beloved Parkside. The all-action wingman was a favourite of the crowds at Parkside, becoming known simply as 'Ahr Freddie'.

'Cec' Thompson signed for Hunslet after being spotted playing in a local workshops competition at Parkside. Cec was bursting with raw energy in his early days at Parkside and he later admitted that, at first, he knew little of what was happening around him. His natural talent was soon harnessed and he gained international honours with Great Britain playing in two of the Test matches against New Zealand in 1951.

Cec was later transferred to Workington and on retirement was one of the driving forces behind the formation of the Student Rugby League. Cec recently wrote his life story in the acclaimed book *Born on the Wrong Side*.

Granville James was a shrewd signing from Newbridge Rugby Union club in 1949. The strong running loose forward played 180 times for Hunslet, scoring 5 tries, and was capped 5 times by Wales.

Hunslet at Wigan's famous Central Park. From left to right, back row: Whitehead, Jones, Metcalfe, W. Burnell, Bowman, Carroll, Newbound, Griffiths. Front row: Talbot, Williamson, Williams, Anson, A. Burnell.

Alf 'Ginger' Burnell was one of the many
fine players Hunslet had during the 1940s
and '50s. Ginger was capped by Yorkshire,
England and Great Britain during his
career with the Parksiders.

The England XIII for the game against France at Headingley on 11 November 1950. Ginger
Burnell is second from the left on the back row. England won the game 14-9 in front of a crowd
of 22,000.

Ginger Burnell shakes hands during the pre-match ceremonies prior to the Great Britain v. New Zealand Test match at Odsal Stadium, Bradford. Alongside him is his Hunslet team mate Cec Thompson.

GEOFF GUNNEY

Hunslet - Yorkshire - Gt. Britain

1960

1/-

Geoff Gunney was one of the finest players Hunslet ever produced. He signed in 1951 and by the time he retired in 1973 had made 625 appearances (including 10 as a substitute), a record that will probably never be beaten. During that illustrious career he was capped by Yorkshire, England and 11 times by Great Britain. Following the sad demise of Hunslet in 1973 it was Geoff Gunney who was the driving force behind the resurrection of the New Hunslet club that played at the Elland Road Greyhound Stadium.

Edgar Meeks presents Geoff Gunney with yet another international cap.

Geoff Gunney is on the far right of the back row of the Great Britain team for the match against France at Knowsley Road, St Helens in April 1957.

A typical Gunney try at his beloved Parkside: Geoff dives over the line despite the attentions of two Wigan defenders.

Hunslet are presented to the Lord Mayor of Leeds at Parkside in 1951. The Mayor shakes hands with Ginger Burnell while Freddie Williamson waits his turn.

A Hunslet team with some of the finest players of the era captured at Castleford in 1956. From left to right, back row: Gabbitas, Shaw, Smith, Hatfield, Poole, Langton, Gunney. Front row: Stockdill, Talbot, Snowden, Clues, Burnell, Preece.

Players from the first and second teams relax after a training session on a field at the side of the Middleton Arms.

Hunslet's new Welshmen Terry Robbins and John Griffiths show their athletic prowess at a press call at Parkside in 1959.

Jim Stockdill dives for the line at Parkside. The Hunslet players in the background are Hatfield, Tare, Clues, Shaw, Gunney, Poole and Gabbitas.

The 1958/59 season was one of Hunslet's finest since the Second World War. The Parksiders finished in third place behind Lancashire giants St Helens and Wigan, winning 27 games, losing 8 and drawing 3 – a total of 57 points. The Parksiders' full-back Billy Langton had a brilliant season, kicking a total of 380 goals to create a Hunslet record that still stands today. In the play-offs for the Championship, Hunslet travelled to Central Park to meet Wigan, who had finished just a point above them in the League table. The Parksiders defeated Wigan 22-11, thanks to tries from South African Ron Colin (2), Alan Preece, Jim Stockdill and five goals from Billy Langton. In the final at Odsal Stadium, Bradford, Hunslet were unfortunate to meet a St Helens side at their awesome best and with Tom Van Vollenhoven scoring a hat-trick of tries for the Saints they were defeated 44-22. That particular final is often recalled as one of the code's all-time classics and, although beaten, Hunslet contributed well to a thrilling game famous for the open play produced by both sides.

THE NORTHERN RUGBY FOOTBALL LEAGUE

League Championship Final
1959

HUNSLET v. ST. HELENS

SATURDAY
16th MAY
1959

Kick-off 3.0 p.m.

At ODSAL STADIUM
BRADFORD

OFFICIAL SOUVENIR PROGRAMME   -   Price 6d.

GIDEON SHAW, PRINTER, CASTLEFORD

The programme cover for the 1959 Championship Final. Jim Stockdill, Kevin Doyle, Geoff Gunney and Harry Poole scored tries for the Parksiders and Billy Langton kicked 5 goals.

112

Eight
The Sixties and Closure

EMPIRE STADIUM · WEMBLEY

RUGBY LEAGUE FINAL
Saturday May 8, 1965
KICK - OFF 3 p.m.

YOU ARE ADVISED TO TAKE UP YOUR POSITION BY 2.30 P.M.

Bracewell Smith

CHAIRMAN:
WEMBLEY STADIUM LTD

EAST ENCLOSURE   **5/-**

ENTER	ENTRANCE
C	13
TURNSTILE	

STANDING

TO BE RETAINED   (See Plan & Conditions on back)

A ticket for the 1965 Challenge Cup final

The 1961/62 season was hardly a successful one for Hunslet. They finished in twenty-fifth place, having won just 10 games, drawn 1 and lost 25. From left to right, back row: Shelton, Langton, Hartley, Eyre, Adams, Stockdill, Gunney. Front row: Newall, Gomersal, Walker, Gabbitas, Preece, Moyser. One bright spot of the season was the selection of Gabbitas and Gunney for Yorkshire against Lancashire at Hilton Park, Leigh.

Hunslet prop Ken Eyre races for the try-line at Parkside. Supporting him are Brian Gabbitas, Billy Langton, and hooker Bernard Prior.

Bill Ramsey made his Hunslet debut towards the end of the 1961/62 season. He left Hunslet in the mid-sixties and went on to become one of the game's greatest second-row forwards, making 5 Wembley appearances and touring Australia and New Zealand with the Lions in 1966. Bill made 15 appearances on the tour and scored 5 tries.

Hunslet in their myrtle, flame and white shirts in the early 1960s. From left to right, back row: Lee, Ramsey, Whitehead, Langton, Eyre, Sam Smith, Hartley. Front row: Garforth, Preece, Shelton, Stevenson, Walker, Robinson. Hooker Sam Smith was a member of Great Britain's first ever World Cup squad in 1954.

Vastly experienced international half-back Jeff Stevenson joined Hunslet from Leeds in January 1962 and played a total of 65 games for the Parksiders. He is shown here scoring one of his 17 tries for the club, beating Wakefield Trinity's full-back, Gerry Round, to touch the ball down.

The 1963/64 season was a great one for Hunslet. The Parksiders were Second Division champions, gaining promotion to the First Division at the first attempt. They were successful in 22 games, losing just 4, and scored 508 points to 214 against. From left to right, back row: Eyre, Ramsey, Ward, Griffiths, Hartley, Whitehead, Preece. Front row: Langton, Gabbitas, Thompson, Prior, Stevenson, Shelton.

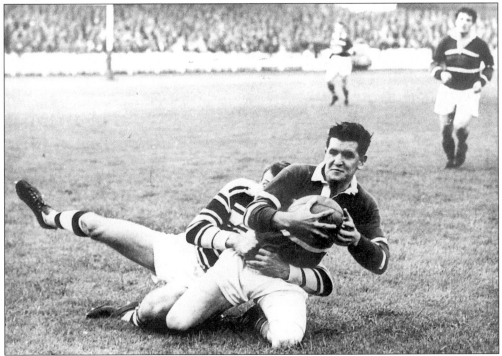

Geoff Shelton was a classy centre who gained honours with Yorkshire and Great Britain. He was a member of the 1966 Lions party to Australia and New Zealand, playing 13 games and scoring 4 tries.

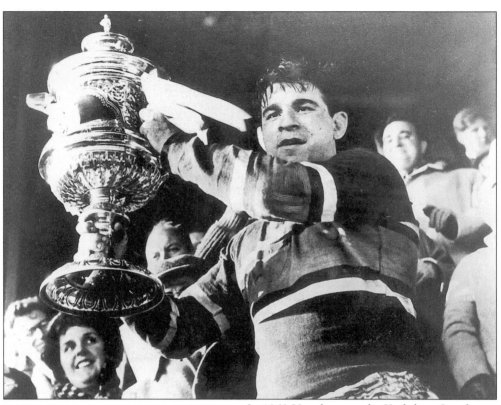

In 1962 Hunslet won the Yorkshire Cup for the first time since their 'All Four Cups' season of 1908. The Parksiders began the campaign at home to Wakefield Trinity, swamping the Dreadnoughts 34-9, then beat Hull 18-7, again at Parkside. Halifax were beaten 7-6 at Thrum Hall in the semi-final and the stage was set for the final at Headingley. A crowd of 22,742 gathered for the eagerly awaited final against Hull Kingston Rovers. Tries from Billy Baldwinson and Geoff Shelton, a brace of goals from Billy Langton and a surprise drop goal from prop Denis Hartley sealed the game for the Parksiders. Captain and coach Fred Ward holds the trophy aloft for the thousands of Hunslet supporters in the crowd. Ward had only been at the club a matter of weeks, but his coaching skills had made a tremendous difference to Hunslet's performances and general outlook to the game.

The cover of the 1965 Yorkshire Challenge Cup final programme.

A superb caricature of Alan Preece, used to illustrate the cover of his benefit brochure.

A relaxed Hunslet team from the mid-1960s pose in front of the cricket pavilion at Parkside. From left to right, back row: Gunney, Taylor, Baldwinson, Ward, Hartley, Griffiths, Prior. Front row: Gabbitas, Preece, Shelton, Marchant, Lee, Langton. Inserts: Hartley, Eyre. Hooker Bernard Prior had joined Hunslet, from Leeds, in 1961. A vastly experienced player, he had been a member of the Leeds side that had beaten Barrow 9-7 to win the Challenge Cup at Wembley in 1957. Fred Ward joined Hunslet at the beginning of the 1962/63 season as player-coach. The ex-Castleford and York forward soon adopted a playing style that was both innovative and successful. Hunslet's tactics were based on a solid defence and controlled football – a method still used by many clubs today. Ward played a total of 106 games for Hunslet, before leaving the club in 1967, having led the Parksiders to Wembley, a Yorkshire Cup final victory, the Second Division championship and First Division safety.

A tug-of-war during training at Parkside.

Geoff Gunney leaves a trail of battered defenders in his wake for another Hunslet try at Parkside. Congratulating Geoff are Brian Gabbitas, Bernard Prior, John Griffiths, and Billy Baldwinson.

The quarter-final of the 1965 Challenge Cup competition threw up a dream game – Hunslet v. Leeds at Parkside. The Parksiders had beaten Oldham and Barley in the first two rounds and, although lying in mid-table in the league, were quietly confident of beating their rivals from Headingley. Hunslet were without Ramsey and Eyre for the match, but helped by a brilliant display of hooking from Bernard Prior they beat Leeds 7-5 with a Griffiths try and 2 goals from Billy Langton. Leeds stand-off Trevor Holroyd is shown here being stopped in his tracks by the Hunslet defence.

Hunslet were paired with the mighty Wakefield Trinity in the semi-final at Headingley. Trinity were riding confidently on a seventeen-match winning streak and were firm favourites to beat lowly Hunslet. The Parksiders' success lay in their massive pack's ability to gain all-important possession and throughout the game Denis Hartley and Bernard Prior were a constant worry to Wakefield. Opposing wing men Barry Lee and Gert Coetzer are shown here standing toe-to-toe as a Hunslet attack breaks down with a fine tackle.

Despairing dives from Gunney and Preece fail to stop a Wakefield Attack.

For over an hour there was no score in the tense game, but then Alan Preece latched onto a loose ball and crossed the line unopposed. A late try from Griffiths and a goal from Billy Langton gave the Parksiders a surprise – but well deserved – 8-0 victory. Geoff Gunney is partly grounded in this action shot, but he still turns to pass.

Billy Langton joined Hunslet in 1953 after a successful spell as the Hunslet Schoolboys' captain. Within two years he had settled into first team football and by 1958/59 became the second player to score in every game of a season. Billy played 44 matches the campaign and scored 6 tries and 181 goals – a total of 380 points. These marvellous achievements still stand as club records today, alongside his total of 1,044 goals for Hunslet and 2,202 points.

Wembley-bound, a group of players relax with a game of cards on the train journey. From left to right: Fred Ward, Bernard Prior, Alan Marchant, Kenny Eyre, Brian Gabbitas and Alan Preece.

The players trained at Worcester Park, London before the final and visited the London Palladium on the eve of the game. The players and officials visited the Empire Stadium on the Friday before the final in an attempt to calm any pre-match nerves.

Fred Ward introduces his players to Her Royal Highness Princess Alexandra during the pre-match ceremonies. Twenty-one year old Bill Ramsey (far right) looks a little nervous but at his side Kenny Eyre manages a wry smile for the camera.

Wigan's Brian McTigue rolls to the ground as he is confronted by a wall of Hunslet players – from left to right: Marchant (7), Ramsey, Hartley, Preece, Eyre, Gunney and Ward. Wigan took the lead in the very first minute with a penalty goal from Gilfedder. The early score upset the Parksiders' game plan of playing a close, tight game centred around their heavyweight pack and when the Wigan backs began to open the game out Hunslet had little option but to play the same expansive game. The result was one of Wembley's classic finals that is still recalled as one of the best ever.

The sheer strain of concentration is etched into the face of Brain Gabbitas has he sweeps round a Wigan defender. 'Gabby' had a fine game that culminated in a joint win, along with Wigan's Ray Ashby, of the Lance Todd Trophy for Man of the Match. This was the first and only time that the prestigious award has been shared.

Despite coming so close, Hunslet were defeated by Wigan but far from disgraced. Fred Ward and Brian Gabbitas pose with Welsh Rugby Union star Cliff Morgan after the game.

The line-up for the last game at Parkside on 21 April 1973. In the late 1960s and early '70s the club was hit by a number of disputes by the players. Attendances were dwindling to figures below 1,000 a match and the problems on and off the pitch were creating a bad atmosphere within the club. At the same time secret moves were being made to sell the Parkside ground. During the early 1970s a series of share issues as well as public and shareholders' meetings culminated in the sale, in late 1972, of Parkside to a development company. Hunslet played their last game at the ground the following year and to all intents and purposes Hunslet Rugby League Club was no longer in existence. However, Geoff Gunney refused to accept that the club could die and along with a group of other people agreed terms to play at the Leeds Greyhound Stadium and launched 'New Hunslet' in time for the following season. The ruinous state of the pavilion in this photograph poignantly illustrates how a rugby league club was simply left to die. From left to right, back row: Ward (physiotherapist), Taylor, Sanderson, Dobson, Sykes, Griffiths, Adams, Chadton, M. Plenderleith (secretary), C. Plenderleith (director). Middle row: Barron, Richardson, Watson, G. Clark, J. Clark. Front row: Horrocks, Gunney, Rycroft. York won the game 22-5, Dobson scoring the last Hunslet try and Adams kicking the last goal. Geoff Gunney was the last Hunslet player to leave the pitch.

Every year since the demise of Parkside an annual reunion of players who were connected with the club gathers in Leeds. Once described as the most exclusive sporting club in the world – you have to have played for Hunslet at Parkside to attend – the gathering of old friends and colleagues is one of the truly moving events in the world of Rugby League Football. In 1983 members of the famous 1965 Wembley squad were captured together again. From left to right, back row: Shelton, Render, Gunney, Hartley, Eyre, Ward, Griffiths, Ramsey. Front row. Baldwinson, Marchant, Langton, Preece.

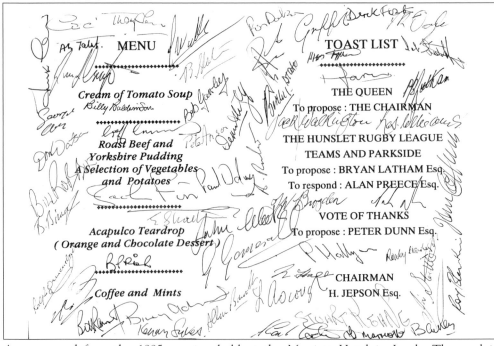

A menu card from the 1995 reunion held at the Marriott Hotel in Leeds. The card is autographed by some of the finest players ever to grace Parkside.